Just Su

Su Laws Baccino

Just Su

Poetry and Prose

dibleydo

First published in 2006

dibleydo

© Su Laws Baccino 2006

The right of Su Laws Baccino to be identified as the author of this work has been asserted by her in accordance with the Copyright, Designs and Patents Act 1988.

All Rights Reserved

No reproduction, copy or transmission of this publication may be made without written permission. No paragraph of this publication may be reproduced, copied or transmitted save with the written permission or in accordance with the provisions of the Copyright Act 1956 (as amended).

ISBN:
0-9553656-0-0
978-0-9553656-0-7

Printed and bound in Great Britain by:
Proprint
13 The Metro Centre
Welbeck Way
Peterborough
PE2 7UH

Cover
dibleydog's view of the river © Su Laws Baccino

Contents

Roots:	Do me a favour – make sure I return	1
	Siberian Slaughden	2
	River Wall	3
	Absolute Farewell	4
	Zealous Power	5
	Onshore	7
	Solitary Land	8
	Under Walserwig's Veil	9
	Local Folk	11
	North Sea Night	12
Life:	Yearning	14
	Searching	15
	Rebelling	16
	Passing	17
	Vanishing	19
Thoughts:	Baby Face	20
	Baby Rebel	21
	Dark Dark Endless Dark	22
	Mistaken Holiday	23
	Saved by a Camel	24
	Teddy Boy Trouble 1956	25
	A change of heart	26
	Forgotten Corner	27
	The Jug	28
	Manipulation	29
Flash fiction:	'Grandpa please tell me the story of 12/11'	30
Short Story:	Feverish Encounter	32

Do me a favour – make sure I return

Green underfelt hosts a carpet of daisies
soon to be lost as Brian mows the field.
Bees bicker in early blooms, birds swoop.
Gentle lapping in river bank
nothing seen – all concealed.

Rhubarb sprouting in allotment;
clematis clings to garden huts
newly painted – blue and green and brown;
watched by scarecrows newly built
mother's old hat, dad's dungarees.
Fresh manure perfumed air
cattle sway against fence;
sheep move as one, like a shifting cloud
as shepherd moves them along.
Young hunter passes by,
shotgun disabled,
returns later with pigeon,
dripping blood.
Birds soar in pavonian sky
wiped with cotton wool clouds;
the sun so bright, so warm, so welcome.
Dog walkers whistle and call;
wave and smile at Brian as he stops
at green dyke for a mid-morning break,
bringing the field to a halt.
And in the stillness, across the way,
balanced on old telegraph wire, a cuckoo calls.
I think I've found heaven.

Siberian Slaughden

Cruel Eurus vents his anger,
blows icy blasts,
whips the waves;
white horses pitch on empty beaches.
Gulls crouch by boats.
Wind moans through awnings,
whistles in the rigging;
tortured flags flap free.
Inn sign dangles in the transom,
throbbing in its creaking.
Dogged winter grips.

Muffled visitors' eyes weep,
bones chilled, hurrying home;
tea and crumpets toasted
by the roaring open fire.

Surrounded by the savage storm
above the tumult of the tempest,
defiant – Orfordness;
beaming warmth, embracing all.

River Wall

In hoarsely blowing breeze I walk the wall
dividing sea from river; salt spray on my lips,
dries, burns. The river's on the ebb.
Receding ripples swept back with whispers,
reveal scooped out caves in the chocolate mud.
Staccato sounds rattle in the rigging,
telling passionate sailors of mounting winds.
Old buildings nestling in the marshes
glow sun-drenched at the end of day.
Ducks, in formation, fly past.
Dodging dragonflies, I'm homeward bound
blinded by the sunset in the outgoing tide.

Absolute farewell

The sea summoned me; fog entombed the coast.
Hesitating, taking my bearings, goat-stepping
down the rock face; steep, dangerous
path that plunged towards the bidding mournful cry.
Pounding waves washed, mortared the shingle,
echoed in my ears – drums, a washboard,
nature's skiffle on the shore. With each stride
the song grew louder, the pace grew quicker, until,
at last, balm hinted at the nearness of the beach.
Gingerly, crossing the divide where verge,
under drifting two-way miasma,
merged with barren land, pebbled mountains;

Closing in on my soulless bidding sycophant,
temptress – impatient, pawing water.
Distant white crests, the sea gallops in;
clouds, pure sheepskins, rise, yielding to Nature,
as the sun bursts through to brighten the day.
From the foothills, frisky wild horses
crowding the beach for their daily fun.

I remembered his ashes scattered
on the outgoing tide, to ride the waves forever.

Zealous Power

A silky mist, cloaked in luminous pall,
floated over the cemetery at dawn,
unveiling scary stirrings at such an early hour.
Creaking coffin lids lifted,
pushing the earth above them, mole-like,
then fell, forcing fetid air from within.
Moribund the contents crept out dropping traces,
slithers of decomposed flesh caught on rusty edges.
Cadavers, unfortunate witnesses, heeding a call
for proof of greedy destruction;
the station had called them to work
then killed them off all in the name of power.
Now they wanted to build more –
Stations . . . power stations . . .

A silent knot of stumbling bones,
they played their way towards the east,
up and over the hill to meet at the coastal site.
A desolate place, a deserted beach
washed by a bubbling, boiling sea.
A delphinium sky pocketed the stillness,
heralding a stifling day.
Wind-chimes in an irregular wind
they clattered on, no time to stop.

A sudden powerful breeze blew in –
they rattled on, castanets on pebbles.
A syrupy smell filled the air,
belching from the chocolate factory,
or so they thought.
Silent gulls floated on a sombre sea;
beyond the rig, on the horizon,
a burning cauldron glided quickly
over the sea; on to the shore
tossing its searing heat.

Sizzling burning bodies, plunged into the sea,
the sickly smell explained –
roasting naked skin and crumbling bones.

Onshore

A cowed vertigo covered the marshes;
asparagus fish tank slime wrapped
coastal defences, joining the dykes,
where trees bent weeping sticky ochre
droplets onto strands; straws of grey blue
woven webs, traps, feeding, sucking it up.
Nature impotent, flattened between.

Animals knee high pressed from high.
A camouflage cloud hovering above,
its innards disgorged, deflated;
about to drop its deathly shell.

Solitary land

Our village gently pushed onshore
Amongst toothed leaves and catkins.
At its heart, the castle ruins,
the keep, on rolling mounds,
in open fields – ancient Orford.

Beyond, fateful flat desolation;
silent stones mossed, slimed,
in dykes, dunes and drifts . . .
scattered cattle graze.

Long dark horizontal line,
rivers Ore and Alde deign to meet;
behind, another low leaden line,
less black – the King's Marshes.

Far off in the western sky,
across Havergate, the avocets' sing, silhouetted
against rows of sinister cadmium, copper, madder
hanging heavy on the savage sea.
All around, yet far away, distant,
isolated voices call.

Under Walserwig's Veil

A forgotten railway crossing and a swinging bridge,
clattering pontoon chain ferry and a scary whistle,
secreted ghostlike in sharpened memory banks;
not destroyed, not dulled, becalmed yet wide awake.

The scented copse, a playroom, for phantom shadows
unseen on dreary *bouffant* sheep that move eerily as one.
Across the way, the ruined church and shocking hush,
the healthy smell of staring, swaying cows that trample
sunken sepulchres and shattered stones;
sad souvenirs of a native folk and a peaceful vibrant port.

In huts once used to kipper herrings, geese squat
as empty odourless shacks on stilts
reflect in the sunbathed river.
Cheerful colours splashed on toy-like dwellings
visible from the sea.

A rotting figurehead off an ancient wreck
pressed onto rocks by hideous winds – moves.
Did I hear the beat of a distant heart?

The name-board of an ill-fated smack,
rolled in a calm North Sea,
lies wrapped in salt-stained sails,
ragged – no sign of telltales.
Is that why it foundered on the sands
or was it the cloaked clout in the tail of a tell-tale cloud?

Coastal yarns narrated by an old raconteur down at *The Ship*,
rubbing gnarled joints, tapping knotted stick, drawing on
                                                      his pipe.

A groan of grief as he tips his cap recalling pain,
pausing to rest his aching, pounding heart,
dead tears drowning his eyes;
recalling lost relatives and friends.
Interrupted by widows and mothers telling tales
of lost lovers that never came home.

Then, taking a cue from the Captain sat at the smoky bar,
they sing merrily with one voice – delicate sea ballads
and melancholy melodies of ships and shipwrecks.

A bygone age revealed, Mediaeval times repeated
in the never-ending saga of man and Nature
under Walserwig's veil.

Local Folk

An ordinary, uncomplicated soul,
that's me. My understated roll
in this terrace, to move among
humble people (unsung
like you and me) who succeed
in average daily deeds.
Save, Fred, he nearly got life,
did away with his wife.
Brenda, tight-lipped, is extremely stupid.
Jilly and Jimmy's fifteen kids,
five prematurely dead.
Betty houses strays and the underfed.
Tom's on benefits, no one knows why,
but he's probably work shy.
Rosie owns the corner shop, Jack,
husband, deals out the back;
and Maria's house is painted purple, papal,
it's something to do with the gospel.

Extraordinary folk.

North Sea Night

The wind swept the chimney
blowing embers on the mat;
Father rose to stamp them out,
'Light the candles, Mother,
there's a rare tempest blowing in tonight.'

Cutting through the dark,
crossing cobbles in the yard,
he fought the storm, to check the horses –
restless in the stables;
pigs and fowl too,
were bunching, moving.
Piled high the sandbags, checked the bolts,
roped and tethered all he could.
Stared at the power lines moaning in the gale
hefty poles challenged, creaking, swaying madly;
he wondered if they'd snap.

Battleship clouds scratched the pitch sky.
Maroon exploded, sliced the air . . . 'the lifeboat – launched!'
Mountainous sea,
purple plunderer of the shingle – ravaged,
wreaked havoc on the shore.
Sacked and sunk the coast road,
swallowed the marshland;
sprinted to meet the bloated river
offering up bones and remains all too human.

Muted, men and women wait –
anxious, they've seen it all before.
Flooded fenland ready to mate with angry sea.

The ticking clock's hands click round,
the ebb arrives, the waters recede.
Father sighs as ruin retreats;
defiantly murmurs
'You'll not win here.
We'll see you off ag'in and ag'in.'

Strong North Sea dwellers smile again
always mindful of the next
surging swell.

Yearning

A twist, a twirl, sea horses, giant walls
destroy the poorer, chopping, corkscrew waves.
Opaline whorls of water, crafting caves
all dug so deep, sad benthos dark zone calls.
A run, a roll, anxious high tide, it falls
empty beach, at ghostly shadows it raves
quiescent *en passant* reprieves the graves
of sailors seized, whose cries echo the mauls.

Ebbing tide reaching out to snatch freedom,
cuts loose, swallows up clean varnished shingle.
Wounds licked, sunbathes on glistening seashore.
Strong undercurrent covers pebbles, maelstrom
sands, pitted stones play rhythmic jingle
rolling on, pivoting – the tide, my paramour!

Searching

Rebellious.
Challenging.
Purple haze moods.
Sometimes painful
Salty acids
burning the skin
on sore sore lips.
I'm a pebble
with a hole.
Incomplete.
Searching for my centre
moving around on the shore;
then plucked,
carried inland
to new open spaces, meadows
where, like a drunken wasp
at summer's end,
belly full of sweetness,
replete,
I turn eccentric.

Rebelling

seagulls are scroungers, pests
always hungry
brawling, bickering airbursts
squealing skydivers searching debris
littering the shore
greedily awaiting the fish'n'chip queue
then over my rubbish sacks soar
quarrelsome, on cue

a fan I am not
still able I reach for my gun
take a pot shot

Passing

Summer's here, silky sea
soft blowing wind
clean the golden sexy sand
wash pure the pebbles –
and worshippers look to the sky
as they roast under the red hot sun.

Each evening when the sun
goes down, darkness fills the sky
leaving shadows on the pebbles.
Void of wind,
calm at sea,
tracer wavelets through the sand.

Morning dawns, rippled sand
whisked by wind
tussles with the ebbing sea,
deserting mounds of rainbow pebbles
to dry alone beneath the sun
and violet tinted sky.

Noon – kites sail the sky
serene above the sea
driven by a casual wind.
Feet sinking into sand,
squinting eyes at a diamond sun
chasing cords across the pebbles.

Children playing with the pebbles,
parents monitoring the sun.
Idle hands sifting the sand
sometimes glancing at the sky
listening to the bubbling sea
then seeking cover from the growing wind.

Now cold, the wind
is up – down the sun,
camouflage grey the sky.
Rivulets of rushing sand,
across the whispering pebbles
an angry pounding sea.

And so ends summer, wind-whipping pebbles;
ominous aubergine sky, mirroring the inky sea;
shifting sands now grey without the sun.

Vanishing

To the horizon they sailed, geared
for a lazy day's fishing, with fee.
With a wave and a smile they were gone,
disappeared . . .

Into the mist, dense, they steered
casting their long lines with glee.
To the horizon they sailed, geared
as the sun appeared, to protect skins seared
laughing and swigging at a flask of tea.
With a wave and a smile they were gone,
disappeared . . .

Around to the north the wind veered
bothering the sea.
To the horizon they sailed, geared
with lifebelts; crests on the waves reared,
a storm, helpless they sank on their knee.
Just what they'd feared
to the heavens they shouted a plea.
With a wave they slipped away,
disappeared . . .

Baby face

My eyes journey through
soft twists of blonde couching
oval eyes of opal, cerulean centres,
in dark velvet lashes trapped
under bows, delicately flexed.
Sit poised on the bridge,
jump like a skier
glide down the nose *retroussé*;
between balanced pink cheeks
dimpled with laughter. See
delicate mouth open; exposing
lively enamel, lighting
the dark void behind rosebud lips.

Baby Rebel

Messily launched into the life I was given
hung by my feet, slapped on my bottom;
rubbing me dry they tidy my bellybutton;
and camisole me tight like a glove,
celebrate my coming . . . no chance of boredom!

Hungry, empty, I interrupted, dared to scream.
Into my fledgling mouth they shoved
velvet breast oozing warm ice cream.
Stuffed, sickened I dozed
brooding the next twist in this tryst.
But then I remembered and tore
at the bracelet that gripped my wrist.

'This is *my* life!'

Dark dark endless dark

Living daybreak through to night
or as sleeping shadows until dawn;
life was always full of light
until thrown forlorn into a hidden world,
where black clouds
unfurled
pitched high, then low; shrouding
a darker side of life.
Sad without hope
evil, full of mischief
a strangling rope –
without light,
without sight,
blind acceptance.
A sentence.

Wind in the trees, I hear.
Warmth of the sun, I feel.
Newly mown grass, I smell.
Sea salt on my lips, I taste.
But oh how I long to see!

Mistaken Holiday

It's noon and sunshine plays hide-and-seek,
flirting and winking with dancing horizon.
Painting violet shadows across the western bay;
dipping and diving behind *les Alpes Maritimes* –
dazzling diamonds flashing mid-day sun –
before finally falling out of cornflower sky.
Purring pines whisper above cliff-top sentinels
sprinkling dust that flies far on a diffident breeze.
Lithe lizards skate silently up and down rocks,
pausing, heads held high, darting tongues
reaching out to touch torrid air; then slipping,
sliding, dash into cold chinks in marbled wall.
Gnats and mosquitoes hide in purple shade,
come out stinging, fighting and biting,
as goose-pimpled bodies stir on sun-beds,
burnt cracking skins feeling the sudden cool.
Blind eyes squint, searching for missing sun.
Flip flops pulled on, towels wrapped close,
scorched sore feet soothed on cooling sands,
they turn about, head for hotels.
Strange food, bingo, quizzes await, and
another disturbed night on an unfamiliar bed,
listening to revellers and the local beat;
counting the hours, dreaming of home.

Saved by a Camel

Scorched open waste, sterile shifting sands,
where granules whisked by chill night breeze
form Dali-like egg-white spirals.
Bathed in iced moonlight from an inky sky
a land fatigued, a desiccating desert
its impotent air sucked dry by stunted shrubs.
Carcasses, once visited by vultures, left stripped
to dot the silent landscape. Lost nomads,
now parchment in bone-dry earth,
where thorns prickle in the starry frost
at night and wither in the fever of day
amongst albumin twirls turned to meringue, seared.

I'm drawn to palm trees on the horizon
where a train of resting dromedaries
paint a curve on the edge of the world.
'Oasis,' I murmur, drowned out by hyena.
Led by sandgrouse scouring for seeds,
I move forward.
A fox scavenges in the last throes of night,
on the cusp,
nudging dawn.
Velvet horns bob close, as gazelle
and addax seek out the sparse grasses.
Spent, but excited, I collapse at the hooves of a camel;
its eyelashes blink, shielding eyes from the sand,
and, with a curl of its lips, smiles a welcome.

Teddy Boy Trouble 1956

I fancy the boy with the pipes and DA.
I won't quit. I must get it right.
So, gyrating to Hailey's *'Shake Rattle and Roll'*,
I continue training for Saturday's gig,
No partner; no problem, I grab a swivel seat.
Puzzled parents glare as I twist and turn
holding on tight to the typing chair.
Round and round . . .
quicker and quicker . . .
back and forth . . .
this way . . .
that way . . .
carpet's wearing bare.
'Shake Rattle and Roll'
'Shake Rattle and Roll'
Over and over again,
Granny holds her head . . . what a racket!
Record's worn . . . needs a rest.
Off I go again to
'Rock Around the Clock . . .'
'Rock Around the Clock . . .'
Faster, faster,
To and fro . . .
Side to side . . .
Up and down . . .
Cheeks aglow; ponytail flying;
Luminous socks, denim jeans,
Button through cardi, worn front to back.

I'll not be a wallflower! I'll not be a square!
I'll dance 'til that Teddy boy turns to stare!

A change of heart

Troubled, at dawn, I traipsed to the shore;
hobbled on shingle,
paddled in brine,
where sand-laden waves dredged,
bathed, rinsed my sad soul.

My hopeless heart fluttered
as a breeze blew new life
and it tingled and pulsated again.

I lay there still, just a few moments,
raking pebbles until my nails bled,
kissing, embracing my born again roots.

Then turning for home quickening my pace,
I patted my chest, listened to its beat,
ready and eager to crank the new day.

Forgotten corner

Sun bounces on Venetian slats,
breeze ripples in voile curtain;
loose dust takes flight,
hangs in stifling air
until thrown by the next puff,
onto wall to wall books and
Christmas's half spent candles.
Torpid fish float in tepid bowl, yawning
through cobwebbed Murano glass,
as a loopy lamb lobs them shade.
Drowsy in oppressive air,
through vents in the blind, I dream
of stripe-shirted singing boatmen
propelling gondolas along a canal,
vanishing into a dark channel
underbelly of the Bridge of Sighs.
'O Sole Mio' echoes in the wake.

The Jug

Emotional.
Frustrated.
I scream.
The jug's on the ground.
Her jug.
Its many pieces scattered.
It belonged to her.
She's been gone for years
but it's still hers.

In between tears
pushing pieces together
fixing them into a shape –
the hope of holding on to my mother.

Then, ice cold anger
melts
as a blanket of warmth
falls around me and sadness.
The sun flickers, shines through
bouncing and winking off the broken glass.
Now entire, no pieces.
It blinds me.
She's still there.

Manipulation

He smiles, he scowls
He chuckles, then weeps
Long-suffering, frustrated
On a high, plunging low
Anxious talk finding peace
Out and about, driving too fast
In the garden, broken-hearted

Stinging tears

He smokes, he drinks, but doesn't eat
He's here, he's there, he's everywhere
And all because of her

Flooded eyes

'Grandpa please tell me the story of 12/11'

Sunday morning. Dawn was breaking. We were asleep. There was an explosion, followed by another so large that it was heard one hundred miles away, and recorded on the Richter Scale. We were thrown from our beds as windows and doors were blow in; air sucked from our lungs; there was thunder in my heart. The house rocked as if dancing on tectonic plates. The front door lock thrown onto the landing; outside total devastation, the roof curled round the rafters like a sardine tin round its key.

When the second and third explosions came we were thrown to the ground, our chests hurt, we became part of the mounds of debris that filled the garden like a thick uncomfortable carpet. In the distance, whining and screeching of fire, police and ambulance sirens mixed with continuing explosions at the depot. The dogs howled and scrapped anxiously at the furniture, you know, like they do on Bonfire Night. We thought an aircraft had come down.

Across the fields, orange flames bellowing out, climbing high into the sky; giant fireballs thrown 200-300 feet; and all around, thick black acrid smoke, putrid smell of petrol, aircraft fuel and who knows what else. We never heard, nor were we ever told how many people had died; there were undoubtedly many casualties. Stories of lucky escapes abounded; it was from these individuals that we collected the true information about what happened before the blast.

On television chiefs of police, fire, environment queued up to reassure the public; telling us they were treating the incident as an accident, so stemming speculation, nipping conspiracy theories in the bud, or so they hoped.

'We are treating it as an accident, nothing else,' they said. I laughed as they advised to close windows, to stay indoors. What windows? What doors? I set about boarding up.

Your Dad grabbed his camera and dashed off across the fields in the direction of the depot, where they said 60 million gallons of fuel, of all kinds, were stored in 26 tanks. Your Gran didn't want him to go; she cried as he cycled off into the murk. We never saw him again.

Our house lay on the edge of a valley, the mass towered high above the flames and us; black and menacing, a noxious trail of particles moving slowly in the windless air, creating a false ceiling to the heavens. Dark as night; dawn never broke that day. The atmosphere oppressive, ominous, foreboding, foggy with fumes. I said a silent prayer, begging it not to explode above us.

My head ached with a repeated thought, how could they be so sure it was an accident? They could no more rule that in, than rule out a terrorist attack, and yet that's exactly what they were doing. Why?

And then the vortex curled its way in, gathering us up, carrying us on to the new world.

Feverish Encounter

The town had been quiet considering it was New Year, but a storm now raged. The wind funnelled its way down the chimney before thudding into the fireplace with frightening ferocity. I jumped up to stamp on the embers scattered on the fireside rug, and Sam, my old Persian cat, moved quickly back, flicking his tail angrily. The hall door shuddered, and, as I thought, because of a draught. Without warning, a woman appeared. I screamed, horrified, cemented to the spot, unable to move, but no sound came from my mouth. I don't know how she entered my home. Who was she? I didn't invite her. I didn't recognise her, but there was something about her features, her mannerisms. The woman's sudden presence frightened me, but the weather was severe and I was more preoccupied with the flickering lights.

'Don't you have any candles? We use them all the time,' the woman asked.

My gaunt guest seemed unaware of my surprise at her arrival, but could immediately sense my concern at the thought of a power cut. I searched for the candles and she laughed in disbelief when I produced the night-lights. I lit a couple. Her gaze moved to the display cabinet and the familiar sight of a good sturdy candle in an old brass holder; she looked puzzled but stayed silent.

'My girls will've lit theirs by now. Mam can't be doing with'e dark. She gets troubled.'

Who was this woman sitting awkwardly in the armchair; she fidgeted, often looking behind her. I offered her a second cushion but she waved it away and explained that at home they only had "them" indicating the upright chairs. She did most of the chatting, stopping once as the lights went out. 'There now.'

Fascinated, I watched her in the dancing candlelight, interrupting her frequently. Since hitting that big, impassable wall in my family history, many questions had been stored in my mind, and for some unexplained reason, I felt this visitor might have the answers.

'Why have you come here, Maya?' I asked. Even as I spoke, I realised that from the first moment I had set eyes on her, I had known who she was, that her name was Maya; the details were missing, that was all. She ignored my question. Instead, she continued on about her love, Joe, her eyes twinkled as she described him; her moody features seemed to come and go as the candle flames blew this way and that sending spirals of smoke into the cool atmosphere. I stoked the fire.

Their families had been determined to keep them apart. Maya smiled mischievously as she recounted how she'd been sent away as a resident domestic with a chemist's family, only to find that Joe, a blacksmith, had found himself a shop in a parallel street. From her attic room she looked down on his poor home. Nine months later Maya returned to her parents. Her family stood by her and together they bore the shame of an illegitimate birth. Everyone knew whose baby it was. Joe was a frequent visitor. Were there tears in her eyes? I couldn't be sure.

Torrential rain now lashed the windows and Maya trembled as she watched the giant whorls of water running down the glass.

'It killed my Mam's spirit. Got too much.' She held her head high, proudly, but now I could see big tears rolling down her cheeks, collecting on her upper lip.

I could think of nothing to say.

'Five. One after the other, I had.' Maya sighed.

'Five babies?'

'Five daughters,' she smiled, remembering them.

'And you never married?'

'Joe couldn't.' Maya twisted her hair, changing the subject, 'I hate storms . . . and floods?'

'Let's get something warm to eat,' I suggested, moving towards the kitchen. 'How did you get here Maya?' I tried.

My words fell on deaf ears. Maya ignored me and continued talking as we settled in the kitchen, but went silent as I flicked the switch on the electric kettle. She watched curiously as the steam wound its way up into the cooker hood. I lit the grill and pulled some steak from the fridge. She took a step back and gasped, clasping her cheeks with her hands.

'What's up? Don't you eat meat?'

Maya laughed. 'Of course I eat meat. That must'a cost a fair bit.'

Gasps and cries of delight punctuated her continuing story as she touched and peered closely at the various electrical gadgets. She was too humbled and polite to ask the questions that swarmed inside her head, but couldn't resist turning the tap on and off a couple of times, fascinated by the water that flowed . . . the hot tap, hot water.

I listened, seeing her clearly one moment and not the next. Then she disappeared, but I could still hear her shoes scratching on the kitchen floor; as if she'd come in from the beach.

'Maya?'

Unnerved, I tripped on the rug as I carried the tray into the dining room. The tray floated away from me and as I caught my breath and watched it move across the room, Maya was visible again, putting it down on the table.

'You nearly dropped that . . . good thing I was here.'

Maya bolted her meal. I had no appetite. I felt sick. She thanked me in between large mouthfuls and said she wished her family could have enjoyed it with her.

'You must bring them to visit one day.'

My words prompted an awkward silence for a few seconds and I thought she was about to disappear again. Then, as if recharged by the meal, she chatted on. The deeper into the story the more agitated she became and her concern for her mother and daughters more acute. The weather worried her. She wondered whether the east coast might be suffering the same hideous storm. She didn't like the wind, the menacing seas; she worried about floods.

'My Joe says I'm silly. He says I shouldn't be scared,' she sighed, remembering the day the sea wall gave way. 'The sea's that powerful, that eerie. No one'll stop it. Headstrong it is, got a mind of its own. Sometimes I watch from the dunes . . . it pounds and grinds the shore, never ending corkscrews they are . . . cutting and chopping. The sea's ruthless . . . got no mercy . . . flattens everything in its path.'

Pacing up and down, Maya was in full flood, there was no stopping her and I wondered what it was that had caused this fear.

'You don't live by the coast. You can't understand. There's no stopping the running and rolling of the sea's highs and lows. It's fickle; you never know what it will do next. Sometimes it brings good news, like when a ship comes in. At other times it broods, waiting for a storm, and only the gulls dare float and wait in the stillness when it's like that.'

Stomping up and down the room Maya continued to berate the sea, likening it to a mad man foaming at the mouth.

'The only time I like it is when the tide's going out,' she continued, 'I like the way the foam of the ebb tide washes the shingle and makes the pebbles shine as if they've been polished.'

'That's it, Maya! I remember from my summer holidays how the sea bubbled and fizzed like champagne in the hollows in the sand as it dragged the shingle with it, back down the beach.' The memory had moved something within me. I was beginning to feel extraordinarily close to this woman.

Then the spell broke. Sam stretched and rose. I opened the door and he shot out, taking a detour round the room, behind the settee. The wild weather invaded our warm space. A cool chill crossed my spine as I closed the door.

Maya noticed me shiver. Extreme cold enveloped me, I was surrounded by freezing fog, but I knew that couldn't be – I was indoors.

Unbowed by the sudden freeze Maya went on talking. How could she not notice the cold, she wore only a flimsy shirt and skirt. If I was cold, she must surely be.

Sam entered through the cat flap in the kitchen and determined to avoid our visitor, shot across the room to the safety of his box, tail whisking the air, ears back, his eyes sharp and focused. He was usually friendly; this was strange behaviour on his part, but who could blame him, I thought; Maya was no ordinary visitor.

Maya moved gracefully; peering closely at everything, checking each object. The books fascinated her, she fingered their spines, almost caressing them but she was too frightened to remove them from the shelf.

'I've got a Bible, er, I mean, I had a Bible,' she offered.

'What happened to it?'

'I don't know, it floated away with everything else. I found Mam and the girls, but that's all. I lost everything. Something happened.' Sadness crept fleetingly across her face. 'I haven't found Joe but I know he's looking for me.'

'I knew *you* were looking for me and I came, so I'm sure to find Joe soon. He'll come.' She paused to study a framed copy of my family tree. Her long fingers traced the longest branch, the one with the brick wall. How fascinating, I thought, it would be to know more about Maya, to trawl back through her history.

'How did you know I was looking for you?'

Then, once again ignoring me, she pointed to a photograph of my husband, 'He's handsome. He looks like Joe.'

'Tell me about Joe, Maya.'

'Why? Do you care?' Maya glared at me – her eyes now dark and hostile.

A bitter gust of wind rattled the letterbox before roaring down the hallway like an express train as Maya disappeared. I expected her to reappear, but this time she'd gone. It was now up to me. The decision was mine. I could follow her or forget her.

I wanted to shout 'Wait for me! I'm coming with you!' But, like the night's bonfires, my throat was dry and spent. And then I noticed it – an old and much used Bible lying on the hall table. I opened it. The name *"Maya Hamond"* looked back at me from the title page.

'Maya, I've found your Bible!' I shrieked.

As I opened the front door a giant wall of water crashed down on my home. The sea rushed in and reclaimed the water with one giant flat-bellied undertow, sucking everything back to the dark abyss from where it had come. Horrified I watched as Sam, still in his basket, floated past me on this outgoing tide. I wiped the salt from my eyes, fighting to stay upright as the strong undercurrent tore at my feet, trying hard to pull me to my death; how much longer could I hold on?

'Where've you been woman? I've searched everywhere. Stay there! I'm coming,' bellowed a distant familiar voice.

The decision was no longer mine . . . I was being called . . . I had to go . . . I stepped forward into the unknown with a Bible, Maya's Bible. Squinting at the darkness, I let the surge carry me through the water towards the voice. Strong recognisable hands stretched out to deliver me to the safety of a large cushioned seat where Sam lay, his big tangerine eyes fixed on me. I stroked his long blue coat. He purred loudly. I licked the salt tears off my lips.

'Is the storm over?' I wept.
'What storm? You frightened me gal. I thought I'd lost you.'
Joe, my darling Joe.

Acknowledgement

to family and friends for their

help and encouragement

through the water towards the voice. Strong recognisable hands stretched out to deliver me to the safety of a large cushioned seat where Sam lay, his big tangerine eyes fixed on me. I stroked his long blue coat. He purred loudly. I licked the salt tears off my lips.

'Is the storm over?' I wept.
'What storm? You frightened me gal. I thought I'd lost you.'
Joe, my darling Joe.

Acknowledgement

to family and friends for their

help and encouragement